— UNDERSTANDING & USING —

Monofilament Thread

Including how to set your machine

Rose Lewis

ROSE LEWIS QUILTING

www.roselewisquilting.com.au

Cataloguing-in-Publication is available from the National Library of Australia.
http://catalogue.nla.gov.au

Creator: Lewis, Rose, author.
Title: Understanding & using monofilament thread, including how to set your machine / Rose Lewis;
Designer: Sharon Furlan.

ISBN: 9780995404526 (paperback)
Note: Includes index.

Subjects: Thread.
Stitches (sewing)
Sewing machines.

Other Creators/Contributors:
Furlan, Sharon, book designer.

Author, Writer & Publisher	Rose Lewis
Editor	Rose Lewis
Designer	Rose Lewis & Sharon Furlan
Photographer	Rose Lewis
Front & Back Cover Design	Sharon Furlan
E-book ISBN	9780995404533

www.roselewisquilting.com.au

DEDICATED

This book has been written and dedicated especially for you, Yes "YOU", the present reader of this book.

As without you, who would I be writing this book for?

I am very grateful and appreciative that you have taken the time to pick up and open this book, with the intention that you are eager and enthusiastic to learn how to work with, and also understand, monofilament thread.

Knowledge is one of the best tools to help us to grow within our own personal journey.

Thank you,

Enjoy

and most of all

"Have a beautiful day".

Rose

CONTENTS

INTRODUCTION

I would love to take this opportunity to introduce myself to you.

If you haven't met me before, then my name is Rose Lewis, I live in the lower part of Victoria, which is at the bottom of Australia. I have been sewing for the biggest part of my life, since a young teenager, in some form or another. Children came along, and so I moved into baby clothes, and as they grew the clothes became bigger. I made my first quilt in the early eighties for my eldest daughter. Patchwork and quilting was very new to Australia at that time, and supplies, books and patterns were certainly limited.

Years have come and gone and these days the main type of sewing that I concentrate on is making exhibition quilts. I have won many awards and at the time of writing this, I have been up for Best of Australia twice.

As well as being a textile artist, I am also a teacher of classes, a designer, and a writer, as well as many other things within my very full and interesting life.

I myself use massive amounts of monofilament thread and have done so for over 30 years, so I am extremely confident in bringing you this short book on how to sort out the majority of the issues and fears, that most people seem to have with using monofilament thread, and to teach you how to set your machines tension that will allow you to confidently use this thread.

Some of these fears can relate to peoples machines, their own lack of confidence for using monofilament, and the huge stigma that seems to be associated with this absolutely brilliant thread.

It is my intention and aim here, within this book to be able to disperse all those fears, and leave you with the upmost confidence and knowledge for moving forward within your personal quilting and sewing journey and just loving and using this thread.

One of my techniques that I have specialised in since approx the mid eighties, is a technique where my applique looks like needle turn but is all sewn on the sewing machine.

Within this technique, I use vast amounts of monofilament thread and over the years I have found out which brands work well, which brands are not so good and which brands I would never touch or use due to many different and varied reasons.

The majority of my work is very precise, and the image of this purple clematis flower here has 51 pieces of fabric within this one flower alone. These pieces all have their edges turned under and are attached to each other with using monofilament thread. I must admit that I did need to use tweezers to be able to actually work with this flower.

I often find that when I am in a classroom teaching a class where we are using monofilament thread, many of the students are quite nervous and unsure as to whether they will be able to get their machines to actually sew correctly.

I always allow the first hour of any class where we are using monofilament thread to teach students how to set their machines and tensions, so that they are able to easily and confidently sew with this brilliant thread.

Now on saying this, "every machine" particularly in this day and age are all very different with the way that tensions are set, the pressures on your machine feet, the way that the threads go through machines, etc. This means that what settings and tensions will work on one machine, won't necessarily work on someone else's machine. They will all be different, individual and varied.

So far I don't recall having had any one that hasn't been able to actually get their machines set correctly to have a nice stitch sewing, a great tension, and also the student feeling confident with now being able to use this thread that they have always lived in fear of, but of course, this is what having 30 years of experience with this thread, allows me to confidently teach .

As I work my way through the class, I see the look of unsureness and fear being replaced with smiles, confidence and chatter, as they all now understand how to set their machines to work this thread.

Some times I will need to spend a little more time with a particular student or machine, but we always get there in the end.

Now as this is such a fantastic thread, and as I have found over time with teaching classes, that there is so much apprehension and fear about this thread, that this is why I have now decided to bring this book on just this one subject to you all, so you too, can feel confident with now purchasing, using and loving this thread.

I will take you through the ins and outs and the types of threads, etc, so let's now get started on this new journey within your quilting and sewing life.

I always say,

"knowledge and understanding of what you are doing, using or creating is a very powerful tool when doing something."

MONOFILAMENT THREAD

Firstly, you will of course need some monofilament thread, so let's talk about that first.

There are two brands of monofilament that I personally use.

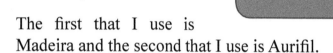

The first that I use is Madeira and the second that I use is Aurifil.

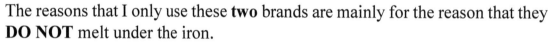

The reasons that I only use these **two** brands are mainly for the reason that they **DO NOT** melt under the iron.
Yes, that is correct, at least for me any way.

There are quite a few brands out there, that when you use an iron on top of your sewing, it will actually melt the thread, or turn your thread very hard and brittle. You won't know this until you are actually using the thread and placing the iron on your work. For this reason alone it is always a good idea when you buy a brand of monofilament thread, to test it out by sewing a little with it, then ironing. I like to be able to iron at the same temperature that I would normally iron for that particular fabric, so if it is 100% cotton, then my thread should withstand the iron set at a hot cotton temperature. The two above brands do.

They should not melt or go hard.

Over the years, I have come across many brands that will melt or go hard under the iron, so if you wish to save yourself lots of money and frustration, then the above two brands should work perfectly for you. Of course on advising this, I would still test it on your work, yourself first.

I have heard some horror stories where people have sewn the entire top of their quilt, then decided to iron it, only to discover that in many areas of their work, the thread had either melted or gone hard. It was very disappointing to them as you could well imagine.

Madeira comes in 2 thicknesses, a 40 and a 60 weight, where the Aurifil is a very fine soft monofilament. I use both the 40w and 60w in the Madeira, with 60 being the thinner or finer of the two.

The Aurifil thread is absolutely beautiful to use, but if you are sewing many thicknesses, as in my quilt here, *"through the garden gate"*, where many of the over lapping and interlocking stems, had up to 10 layers of fabric that I was sewing through, it can be a little fine, so you would be better to use the Madeira in a quilt like this one.

Although on saying this, the Aurifil was absolutely perfect for the very tiny pieces that I used within many of the very tiny flowers around the gate and for the cobblestones that have created the pathway. By using this finer thread, saved having any thread build up within these very tiny pieces, but that would be the same rule applied with using a normal cotton thread.

I actually used a mixture of all three of these threads within this quilt.

Always look at just what you're sewing, and then determine what weight of thread would best suit your area. Just because it is monofilament thread does not necessarily mean that one thickness will suit all areas of sewing, just like cotton thread doesn't.

You need to ask yourself these questions:

Do I need a thicker thread for extra strength, due to the amount of layers I am sewing through?

Do I need a much finer thread, due to the amount of thread build up with sewing many tiny pieces together very closely?

Do I just use a mid range thread like a 60w, as I am only sewing two or three layers together?

Only you will know the answer to these questions as it will be dependent on what you are sewing at the time. You will find that after you have used the monofilament thread a few times, you will easily get to know which thickness to use, just like you would in 100% cotton thread.

I would suggest initially starting off with purchasing a spool of Madeira 60w monofilament, but don't stress if the only weight they have in stock is a 40w, it will be fine. And why you are there in the shop, you may like to purchase yourself a new packet of needles, as you want to make sure that you are starting off with a new needle in your machine.

Smoke or Clear?

Both of these brands of monofilament thread come in both a clear and a smoke colour.

The smoke is supposedly to be used on dark fabrics without being seen. I have personally found after many years of testing, that I can see this smoke coloured thread more than the clear, even on colours like black and dark browns, so I personally do not use the smoke at all.

I have been given new spools, of several different brands to test out for the company/store over the years, and when I have taken my samples of both smoke and clear back to them, they had all agreed that the clear monofilament used on many different coloured fabrics was the better choice.

As always though, everything is just my personal view and everyone has their own personal freedom of choice. Testing for yourself will always give you the most perfect answer for yourself and your project.

I have stood at many quilt exhibitions and done many speaking events, and people, even those that were only a couple of inches away from the quilt, have really struggled to see my thread and stitches. Most people at first believe that I have created my quilt using needleturn.

Sometimes it can take quite a bit of pointing out areas before they are actually convinced that I really have sewn my quilt on the machine using monofilament thread, and yes clear thread on dark fabric too.

This achievement is the result from using a good quality thread, having the correct size and type of stitch for what I am sewing, a good sharp needle and of course the correct tension.

This is the perfect result that you will hopefully achieve within your quilts, when you have finished and practised this book.

A BRIEF OVERVIEW ON WHAT
WE WILL BE DOING

The way that I teach within a class room for, "How to set your tension for using monofilament thread" is........

Firstly, I allow approx an hour to do this. It may take you ten minutes, but for most people it will take a good 40 mins and for some up to an hour, but once you have it, as long as you write your settings down, you won't need to go through all these steps again, unless you are using a very different type of fabric, etc.

Remember, within the actual class room, I am there to help, guide and work with everyone, so if it takes you a little longer then I mentioned above, then don't be too concerned.

Next we find the desired stitch that we want to sew with.
We then will fine tune this, in size.

Then we will work at getting the tension correct.
The way that we do this is to drop your top tension to "0", this then allows you to be able to gradually increase your tension to where it will suit your particular machine.

Your tension will usually end up lower than where you would normally sew with your cotton or polyester thread. Once you have worked out where it suits your particular machine, do make a note of it, so next time you will know just where to set your tension to.

One of my machines I need to alter the tension quite dramatically, while the other machine, I just use it where the tension is normally set to. Do remember,

every machine is different, and that will mean every machines tension setting will be different.

We will only be adjusting the <u>top</u> tension.

Some will say that you also alter your bottom tension, this I have never personally needed to do.

I only use monofilament in the top thread, never in the bobbin.

I always use monofilament with a very tiny appliqué or blind stitch. Some machines have more range than others for finding just the right stitch that will suit your particular needs, some will allow you to mirror the stitch, and then some machines allow you to actually design your own stitches and save into the memory of the machine.

When you are trying to get your tension correct, make sure you are using the same stitch that you will actually be using for your project.

It is also a great idea to actually use fabric the same as what you are going to be sewing. It would not make much sense if you used one type of fabric to sort out your stitch and tensions, had everything just perfect, and then switched over to using a totally different fabric. I usually like everyone to use 100% cotton fabric when doing this, as normally within the class, we are about to work with appliqué using 100% cotton fabric.

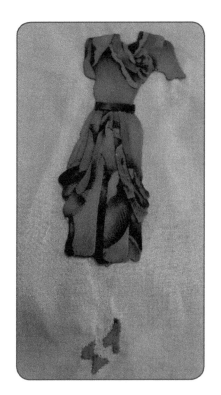

The image here is from my "Lady in Red" quilt and is still in the creating at this stage. All the many pieces of her dress and shoes have all been joined together using monofilament. There are approx 16 pieces to this dress from the belt down and then the shoes consist of 3 very tiny pieces of fabric that have also been joined using monofilament thread.

This small A4 size quilt was made as a challenge quilt for Waverley Patchworkers Bi -Annual show. The criteria for this quilt, was it had to be red and white with a touch of black, and the design and technique choice was totally your own.

As I absolutely love the 20's, 30's & 40's eras, straight away I just knew what I was going to make. Found the perfect piece of fabric, which worked incredibly well for this design. There are 33 separate pieces just within my "lady", all held together with monofilament thread.

I was thrilled to have won Viewers Choice for this quilt, which was the highest award within the challenge quilt category and it was judged with approx 70 other quilts with the same criteria, but different designs.

SETTING YOUR STITCH

If you have an 'open toed' foot for your machine, then I suggest that you use that foot. I use open toed feet for all my appliqué, general sewing and my quilting foot is also, open toed. These are <u>absolutely brilliant</u> for sewing with, as you can really see where you are sewing, particularly when working with monofilament thread, as otherwise it can be very difficult to actually see.

I always suggest within my classes that for those that have never used an open toed foot, then it is well worth spending the money to purchase one. Once you have used them, it would be very seldom that you would go back to your closed toed feet.

Use this one for Applique, etc

Use this one for Quilting

Firstly:
Cut yourself a small approx 8 to10 inch square piece of **plain** coloured fabric.

Fold this in half, and press with your iron.
<u>Do not</u> use a patterned fabric for this exercise, as you won't be able to see your stitches clear enough.

An 8" Square of fabric   *Folded in half one way*

Next, decide on what stitch you will be sewing for your monofilament work, remembering, I personally use an appliqué stitch for all my work. My machine also allows me to totally design the stitch I require myself. Play around with your machine's stitches, to find a stitch that suits you. Check out if it will mirror the stitch as well, as it may be facing the wrong way for ease of sewing.

I prefer to have it so the stitch that crosses over into you fabric, crosses into the left, meaning your fabric will be to the left of your needle. If your machine doesn't have a stitch that goes this way, where it only goes to the right, then this is fine, it will just be more awkward to sew if you are working on a big piece of fabric.

Some of you will find that you don't have an appliqué or a blind stitch and possibly will then need to use a zigzag stitch. The appliqué or blind stitch is the preferable stitch as it has a straight stitch that will sew into your fabric against your appliqué shape; it will then cross over into the actual appliquéd fabric, then back out and do the straight stitches once again.

I talk more about this within my books for learning my appliqué technique.

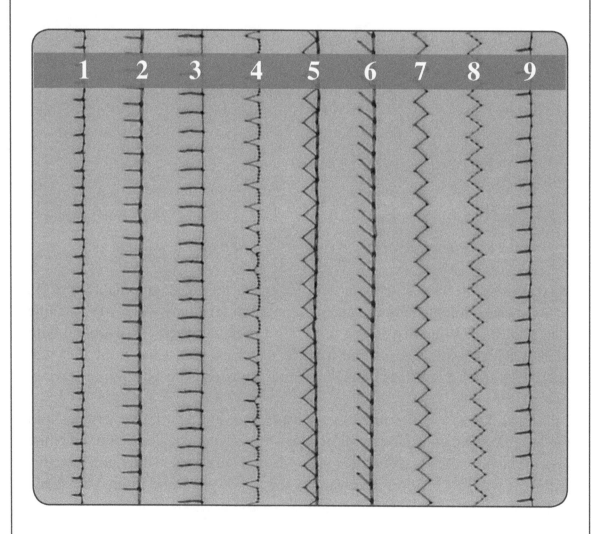

Looking at this image here from left to right, you will see the order of my preferred stitch. Remember every machine is different, and this will just give you a guide to help you find a suitable stitch within your machine. Your machine may only have one or two of these stitches, and that is okay, just choose the one that is the closest to this order of stitches.

Image 1 – Pink on Far Left

The exact stitch that I always use myself. This stitches, as one stitch going left into the fabric and back out again, exactly on top of the ingoing stitch, then it has two straight stitches before crossing back into the fabric.

Image 2 – Turquoise Image to the Right of the Pink One

This is more commonly known as a blanket stitch. Similar to the previous stitch but this has one stitch that goes across into the fabric, and back out on top once again, then it has just one straight stitch, but this sews forward once, then back, and then forward over the top of the stitches again ready to then cross back to the left. This is a really nice smooth stitch but it can create a little bulk with your thread. On saying this, this would be my second choice of a stitch.

Image 3 – Orange Stitching

This stitch is very similar to the first two, but this one has two stitches happening in the cross stitch, then two back down again, and the straight stitch across to the next stitch is just one stitch.

Image 4 – Green Stitch

This is a basic Blind stitch, where the stitch that crosses over to the left into your fabric is more like a zigzag stitch, and then the straight stitch that sews to the next cross stitch is actually several very tiny straight stitches. Sometimes with this stitch you will be able to see the straight stitches a little, just because they are very tiny and close together.

Image 5 – Pink Stitch

This stitch is like a zigzag stitch with a base on it. This is often known as an appliqué stitch. The zigzag goes once up and once down and then the straight stitching will sew a line underneath the zigzag. This stitch gives you a nice straight edge against your appliqué if this is where you are sewing your monofilament to.

Image 6 – Turquoise Stitching

This stitch can be used in certain places, but is not a good choice if you have points and right angles to be sewing around. There are several stitches similar to this one, and the ones that sew downwards, I definitely would not recommend using. This stitch can also create bulk in the straight stitching as it sews back over itself three times. Great if you are doing a heavy thread for feature stitching but not so good for monofilament thread.

Image 7 – Orange Stitching

This is your basic zigzag stitch. I would only use this if you do not have any other choice of suitable stitches if you are attaching appliqué, as you really want a stitch that will finish nicely against your appliqué. If your machine is a very basic machine that possibly only has a straight and a zigzag stitch, then by all means use this.

Image 8 – Green Stitching

This looks like your basic zigzag, but this stitches three times going up the stitch and three times sewing down the stitch. You would be able to see your stitches more easily if you used this stitch.

Image 9 – Pink Stitching on Far Right

This is just a bigger version of image 1, my preferred stitch, just so you can see it a little better. This is a stitch that I created myself on my machine, as my machine allows me to do this, but most machines will have a very similar stitch as this one...It is my suggestion that you try to find a stitch as close to this one as possible, but if not, then just look for something else on your machine that is very similar to the sewn stitches here.

Remember to check out your sewing machines manual, for helping you to find the best suited stitch that your machine comes with. Quite often, we can look at our machines selection of stitches, on the machine itself, and not see a stitch that will suit our needs, but when looking for a stitch within our actual books, it can be surprising at just how many stitches we actually see that may be suitable for our need at the time. I think sometimes when we are really looking for something in particular; our brains seem to pick it up quicker on paper.

So now moving on once again:

Place some darker cotton thread in both your bobbin, and on the top of your machine. Make these two threads both different colours, so you can easily distinguish which one is the top thread and which is the bobbin thread. I normally use an Aurifil 50w for most of my 100% cotton sewing. You of course will have your own preferences of what 100% cotton thread you like to use.

Make sure that you have a new needle in your machine, so you can get the best result possible. By starting off with a new needle, you will know that any tension issues will not then be related to your needle. I would suggest for this exercise that you use a size 70 or 80 needle. I talk a little more about needles further into the book.

Using your piece of folded fabric, you can now sew a row using the stitch of your choice. Once this has been sewn you will be able to look at it and then adjust this stitch, in its length and width, to how you will want your finished stitch to look for the project you are working on.

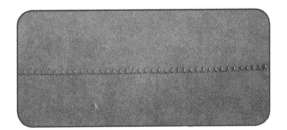

This is the front of the sample

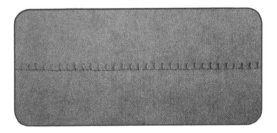

The purple thread is the back

This shows where I have sewn several rows of stitching until I am happy with the stitch.

The reason that we are doing this using coloured 100% cotton thread, is that once you place your monofilament thread onto your machine, it will be very difficult to see the actual stitch. So it is much easier to create the correct stitch, size and length with using thread that can be seen.

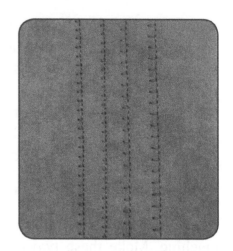

Once you are happy with the stitch, you can then change your <u>"top thread only"</u> to your monofilament thread. We still need the darker bobbin thread on, so we can easily see it when we start to adjust your tension.

SETTING YOUR TENSION

To achieve the correct tension, take your folded piece of fabric once again, making sure you have your monofilament thread in the top and your normal thread in your bobbin and a new needle in your machine.

Next, drop your top tension to **zero, "0"**.
This is one of the most important steps when setting your tension to use monofilament thread.

On that scrap fabric start to sew beside your other rows of stitching.

I generally find it is easier to sew a row first, and then check both the front and back for tension. It may not look too good at the moment, but that's fine.

Tension dropped to "0"

As you start to sew the next row, slowly increase your tension, not much, just a little at a time, as you sew that row. Continue doing this, bit by bit, until you feel that it is right. This may take a little fiddling here, but by taking it slowly and continually checking the back of your fabric, you will easily see when the setting of your tension is almost correct.

I have sewn two rows of monofilament here

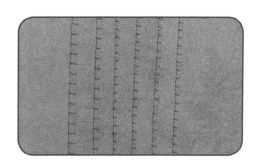

The back showing my tension is correct

You may find it easier to raise your tension a little, sew the complete row, look at the front and back, then make another slight adjustment and sew the next row and continue in this manner until you get it close to looking correct.

Once you have it close to looking correct, then just fine tune it a little more, by either raising or lowering the tension.

You will "see" when it is correct for your machine.

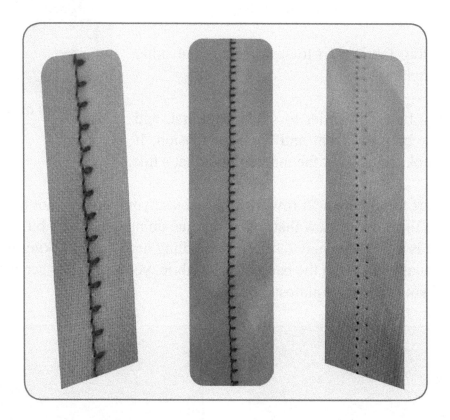

These images here show where I have decided on the required stitch I would be sewing with, and the second image is where I have fine-tuned the size of the stitch I will be sewing with, in both length and width, and then the third image shows where it is now sewn in the monofilament thread.

Do write down the stitch, length and width so you have it for referencing back to at a later date.

The image on the far right is with using monofilament, and although I have placed the purple thread in the bobbin, it isn't actually the thread that you can see, it is actually the needle holes in the fabric. Needle holes will always close up when you next wash your fabric. The image was also taken at close range to give a better view.

Next:
We are now going to be attaching a piece of appliqué to our piece of fabric for the last part of setting our tension correctly.

Do not try doing this next step with raw edge appliqué, as monofilament thread does not work very well with raw edge appliqué. It needs to have the edges turned under, preferably with a stabiliser of some description under it.

If you are doing appliqué as per my method that I use and teach within my classes, or the book on my website at **www.roselewisquilting.com.au** you will now create and place another piece of coloured fabric on top of where you are sewing, just as if you are really attaching some appliqué.

It will only take you a few minutes to create a shape this way.

For those of you who don't know this technique, I will very simply step you through this. Please note, this is not comprehensive of how I do my technique, this is just showing you something very basic, so you are now able to move to the next step for your final adjustment of your monofilament tension.

Trace this shape onto the dull side of a small piece of freezer paper and then cut it out on the line. Iron and cut out another piece of fabric a little larger than the freezer paper shape.

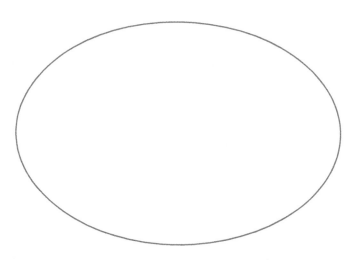

Iron onto the wrong side of fabric

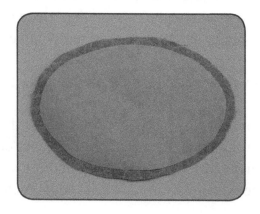

Cut away the outer material

Next, iron the freezer paper, shiny side down, to the wrong side of your fabric. Then cut around the outer edge of the fabric leaving approx ⅛ to ¼" of fabric on the outer edge of this fabric.

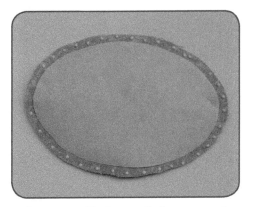

Place small dots of glue on edge

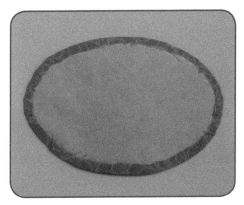

Turn edge over freezer paper

Now place very tiny dots of wash away glue onto the edge of the fabric, then turn the edge of the fabric over the freezer paper.

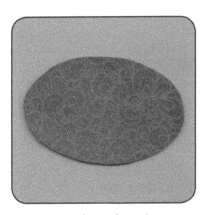

Front of appliqué piece

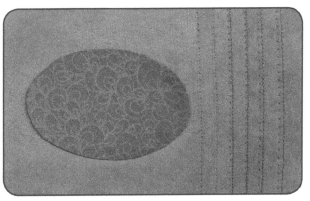

Sitting on fabric ready to sew

Make sure that the edges are flat and smooth, so you will get a good edge for stitching against. You can now sit this shape onto your other piece of fabric and start stitching around the outer edge.

Stitching around the outer edge of the appliqué piece with an open toed foot

Check your tension as you sew, and now make any final adjustments to your tension that may be needed. As this is your final step in setting your tension correct for using monofilament thread. You may find that you need to make a couple of these shapes, as you do the final fine tuning of your tension. Do not settle for second best, make sure it is correct, as by spending another 30 minutes or so here now, you will forever be able to easily sew with monofilament thread always having a brilliant stitch and tension.

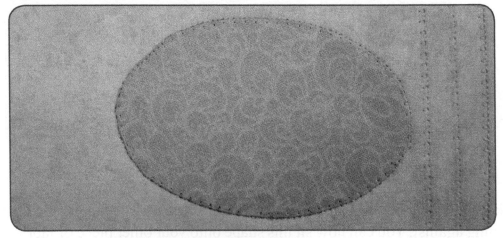

This is now stitched on, having made some tension adjustments as
I sewed around the outer edge.

Once you are comfortable that you now have your stitch and tension correct, make sure that you now write down the tension setting that is showing on your machine. You have done a lot of work here and you don't want to lose all those settings.

I advise my students to write the details of the actual stitch, length and width as you did in the previous step, and also the tension in the inside cover of their machines manual, so they will always know just where to find it for future use. Of course writing it within this book here would be a fantastic place. You will find a page for this, in the back of the book.

You will now be feeling pretty confident about understanding & using monofilament thread within your quilts, as you now have the knowledge for how to set your machine to work with this amazing thread.

DITCH STITCHING

I also use monofilament for my entire ditch stitching within my quilts.

This is achieved with dropping the feed dogs, attaching my quilting foot, putting normal thread into the bobbin and monofilament on to the top of my machine, just as you have already being doing here. The main differences here is that you are dropping your feed dogs, changing to your quilting foot, and sewing around your pieces of appliqué or ditch stitching within the seams of sashings, blocks, flying geese, etc.

If you are wishing to do straight line ditch stitching, then just use your open toed appliqué / sewing foot, as like the one in a previous image, or if using your walking foot, leave your feed dogs raised, and adjust the stitch length to your desired length.

I do not do as much piecing work these days, I concentrate on appliqué and trapunto as this is what I resonate with so much at the moment, but I always, meaning always, ditch stitch around every little shape, etc, regardless of whether it is appliquéd or pieced. Once again by doing this your finished result and masterpiece, will be so much better than you may have imagined. It will give your quilt so much more "definition", "pizazz" and "Wow".

So regardless as to whether you are ditch stitching around your blocks, sashings, flying geese, appliqué, thread painting, fabric painted areas, trapunto, etc, your quilt will really come alive once you have ditched stitched using monofilament thread. Then of course by quilting around many of these areas, your result will be even more magnificent, but that is another subject for another time and book.

Just remember to do a test sample of your tension once again to make sure that it will be correct for this now thicker work. I don't normally have to change mine from its original setting that I worked out as per my earlier instructions, but if you do need to change it, then remember to write it down so you will always have it at hand, for future quick referencing.

If you look at this image here, it shows part of the back of my "a caterpillars dream quilt", which has all been massively trapuntoed throughout the entirety of the quilt, including under the appliqué.

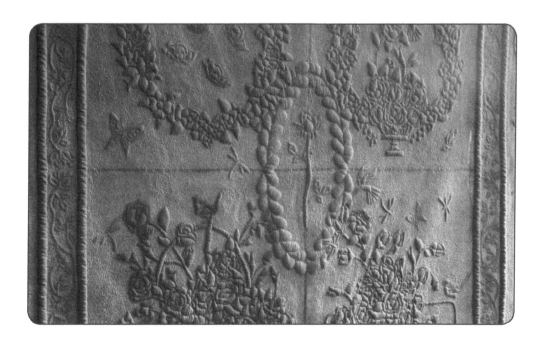

This effect on the back has been created because I choose to ditch stitch all my work, using monofilament in the top of the machine and a matching 100% cotton thread in the bobbin. Do not under estimate the ways and effects of monofilament thread.

You too can achieve these same types of effects by just learning how to set your machine for using monofilament thread.

A FEW MORE TIPS & POINTERS

Always use a matching thread colour in your bobbin, to your fabric backing. I normally use 50 weight, 100% cotton Aurifil thread in the bobbin.

Some will say:
"My machine just doesn't like using it".

Hmmm...It is not so much that their machine doesn't like monofilament thread, but more to the reasoning that these people have not learnt or understand some of the diversities and complexities of using this thread and how to adjust their machine and tension. You yourself, are now well on the way to being able to say to these lovely people, "No it may not be your machine, it may just be that you haven't been taught how to _set your machine to like the thread_".

You will also hear people say, ..."It ruins your machine".

Now as I am **not** a machine technician, I can't really answer this one correctly, but from personal experience, I have never had any issues with this, and one of my previous machines was 16 years old when I changed it over, and it had many thousands of metres of monofilament thread go through it over the years. Never was it a problem.
At the time of writing this, one of my daughters is still using this machine, which is now 25 years old.

A previous sewing machine technician that I used for many years, advised me after asking him once if monofilament thread damages your sewing machine, _"Not that he was aware of as he had never seen a sewing machine that had been damaged by using monofilament thread"._

If it ruins your machine, why do the manufactures make it?
Surely they wouldn't want to be sued.

But do make sure, you use a _very good quality thread_, this is very important.

Using a cheap, poor quality brand of monofilament thread will create so many issues for you, including tension and stitching issues, breaking and tangling of thread, etc, plus the frustration that it will cause you and the time to unpick your work and then to try to sort out why it won't sew perfect, as monofilament does sew perfect when you have your machine and tension set correctly and you use a good quality and brand of thread.

So do yourself a favour, spend the extra few dollars, and take your thread home, and settle in and enjoy sewing.

NEVER, use the thread to the end of the spool.
When it starts to curl, throw it out and start a new spool.
It isn't as wasteful as you think, as it takes a lot of sewing to use a spool of monofilament, remembering that you are also only using this in the top of your machine, so it is like you only use half as much, but if you keep using it to the very end, then you will start to have all sorts of problems with it.

This is normally near the end of the spool, and you "will" realise just when it is time to get rid of it.

DON'T keep it, be brave and throw it in the bin, otherwise you will bring all sorts of grief into your life.

I normally use a very small needle when using monofilament like a 60/8. Generally the work that I am using monofilament for, has many layers of sewing happening within it, where by the time I have finished there could be up to 3 or 4 different types of thread and sewing used on top of each other, and even up to ten layers of fabric, before I actually finish what I am sewing.

For this reason, I do not want any larger needle holes than are needed, as it can stress your fabric. Generally, and particularly if you are using a 100% cotton fabric, your needle holes, regardless of the size of the hole, will disappear when you first wash your quilt. It is just the nature of 100% cotton fabric.

If what I am sewing is very thick, then I will need to go up a size or two, sometimes to a size 90 jeans needle, but generally I like the size 60/8, for this part of my sewing anyway. Be aware that if you have a self threading machine, most machines will not thread an eye of a size 60/8 needle so you may need to thread it manually. If you can't see the thread to thread the machine manually, use a black marking pen, to colour the end of the thread.

Also be aware of the thickness of your particular monofilament, that it is suitable with the size of your needle. If in doubt then use a needle with a bigger eye, as this will sort out some or most of those problems that you will automatically just say... "It's the monofilament"...

Another very important thing is to make sure that you have a needle in good condition in your machine. I find within teaching classes that many issues will relate to a blunt needle, so do yourself a favour and put in a new needle. I love the Superior titanium needles, as these are very strong and being titanium they do not blunten as quickly and they just glide through your work.

So much so, that I know someone who has sewn through their finger, bone and all, needle went up and down twice before the machine stopped, and once the needle was surgically removed, the needle was still in perfect "as new" condition. "Ouch". Now that is what I call a strong needle.

Actually it was one of my beautiful granddaughters who was eight years old at the time. She was fine, as was her finger after a few days, but as for that needle, it was amazing to still be perfectly straight and totally intact.

They are a little more expensive to buy, but they last a lot longer than your normal sewing needles.

If you are using an Applique or Blind Stitch

When setting your stitch size, have the straight part of the stitch quite short, and the stitch that goes across into your fabric, have it where it just catches the appliqués fabric by approx 1mm.

Do make sure that it does actually catch the appliqué as I know by experience just what happens if you have it too narrow and it doesn't catch.

On saying this, you don't want the stitch too wide either as it will then show up on your work too much.

Ideally, when someone looks at your work they should never be able to actually see your stitches, and if you use my appliqué technique, then nine times out of ten, people will think that you have created your personal masterpiece by hand, using needle turn, and not the machine.

Sometimes some people take a lot of convincing that I have sewn all my appliqué on the machine and not by hand. Ideally this is the result that you are looking to achieve with using your new found knowledge from within these pages here, on using monofilament thread. Marry it with my appliqué technique, which you will find on my website at **www.roselewisquilting.com.au** and you are on your way to being able to create the type of results that I myself personally achieve.

Check out this image for where I have sewn the petals of a flower together, to give you an idea of the needed size for the stitch.

If your machine doesn't do an appliqué, a blind stitch, or something similar then you are able to use a zigzag stitch. The monofilament thread will sew the zigzag stitch just as good as when sewing an appliqué stitch etc, but you will find using a zigzag stitch for my style of appliqué will be a little more difficult.

You will find other books within my website that also teaches some of my techniques, etc, for example, you can easily learn how I do my technique of trapunto, where I **do not** cut into the back of my work or thread wools into my work. My technique is simple but very, very effective.

As I said earlier within this book, knowledge is a very powerful tool to have.

Hopefully this book and all the information within its pages, helps you tremendously with your monofilament thread. It will be trial and error at first, but be patient and if you follow these instructions, you should be able to get it to sew perfectly on your machine.

All my students within my classes always leave with a huge new understanding, knowledge and confidence with using and understanding monofilament thread than they had before they entered the class, and I feel very positive that you will also leave this book feeling the same way.

I will leave you here now today, with a little quote to finish, as I am sure that you are just itching to get started on your new learning journey.

To avoid failure,

is avoiding Progress.

Life & progress begins

at the end of our comfort zone.

— (Author unknown)

Wishing you the most amazing day

Enjoy

Rose

INDEX

YOUR CREATED SETTINGS

Stitch Name ....

Stitch Length ....

Stitch Width ....

Tension ....

Notes about this stitch ....

Stitch Name ....

Stitch Length ....

Stitch Width ....

Tension ....

Notes about this stitch ....

Stitch Name ....

Stitch Length ....

Stitch Width ....

Tension ....

Notes about this stitch ....

YOUR CREATED SETTINGS

Stitch Name ....

Stitch Length ....

Stitch Width ....

Tension ....

Notes about this stitch ....

Stitch Name ....

Stitch Length ....

Stitch Width ....

Tension ....

Notes about this stitch ....

Stitch Name ....

Stitch Length ....

Stitch Width ....

Tension ....

Notes about this stitch ....

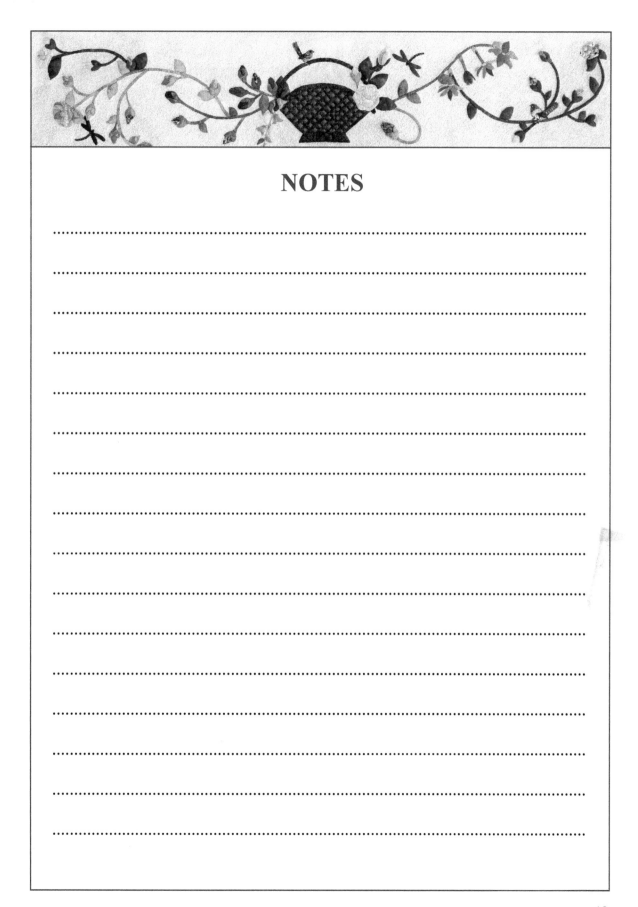

NOTES

....
....
....
....
....
....
....
....
....
....
....
....
....
....

OTHER BOOKS

100 Inspirational Tips to help you on "YOUR" Quilting Journey

Paperback ISBN 9780995404502

100 Inspirational Tips to help you on "YOUR" Quilting Journey

E-book ISBN 9780995404519

Understanding & Using Monofilament Thread
Including how to set your machine

E-book ISBN 9780995404533

www.roselewisquilting.com.au